Dream Journal:

Dream Interpretations, Dream Meanings & Dream Analysis You Can Do Each Day to Finally Understand Your Subconscious

ROZELLA HART

BONUS: BOOK CLUB INVITE

Before we get started with this Dream Journal book, we wanted to tell you how much we appreciate you as a reader, and that we want to invite you to our Free Book Club.

When you subscribe, you get first access to discounted and free new releases from or small publishing house, Walnut Publishing.

Claim your invite at www.walnutpub.com.

Thanks for buying, and enjoy reading.

NOTE FROM THE AUTHOR

Thank you for purchasing "Dream Journal: Dream Interpretations, Dream Meanings & Dream Analysis You Can Do Each Day to Finally Understand Your Subconscious."

I hope you will learn a lot of valuable information that you can apply to your own life, as well as have some fun and be entertained!

I worked hard to write this book with you, my reader, in mind. Whether you enjoyed the book, or you think I got some things wrong, I'd love to hear from you.

I personally read all my reviews on Amazon, and love to hear from my readers. If you can take a minute to just write at least one line about what you thought of my book, I'd be really grateful.

Type this URL into your browser to go straight to the review page for this book: bitly.com/dreamjournalreview

I really appreciate it, and now, let's get to the book!

—Rozella Hart

TABLE OF CONTENTS

1 Introduction

HAVE YOU EVER WONDERED WHAT your dreams mean? We all do. Every night, whether you remember them or not, you have dreams. They may be quite literal, like going through your morning routine and getting ready for work in the morning. (And then you wake up and realize you have to do it all over again!) Or, your dreams may be quite fantastical, taking you on journeys with strange creatures to bizarre lands. Maybe you even fly to get there. Maybe people form your past or celebrities show up. Or new people you have never met! But — what does it all mean?

That is what this book hopes to answer for you. By beginning to pay attention to your dreams and derive meaning from them, you will become better at understanding your subconscious, emotions and your own waking life. We will look at setting the right environment for interpreting your dreams, how to interpret them, provide a dream symbol dictionary that you can reference, and provide you pages to record your dreams. (For the ebook version, we provide you with questions that you can copy answers to in a notebook of your own. In the paperback version of this book, we provide space for you to write your own answers.)

No matter whether you are a beginner or quite practiced in paying attention to your dreams, this book will help you advance your self-study and illuminate some things you never knew about yourself before.

I'm glad you've chosen to take this journey, and I can't wait to help you on your way. Let's get started.

2 How to Remember Your Dreams

For those beginning on this dream journey, you may not remember your dreams that often. The first step to interpreting your dreams is, of course, to remember them!

Thankfully, the best way to begin remembering your dreams is to keep a dream journal, which this book will help you do.

Prepare Before Bed

A great way to remember your dreams more frequently is to remain conscious of your desire to remember your dreams as you fall asleep. Keep a sticky note with a reminder next to the bed, or set an alarm on your phone to remind you each night as you are brushing your teeth and preparing for bed that you want to remember your dreams.

When you lay down to sleep, calm your body with deep breathing, and try to clear your mind. Make sure you have prepared a restful sleeping environment in which the temperature is comfortable, there are no bright lights, and you can feel relaxed and ready for sleep. You can think about a problem or issue in your life you are trying to find a solution to — as long it's not something that will stress you out and keep you up! But often, our brains will work on our problems while we sleep, and this could be a good way to use your dreams.

Go to bed early enough so that you can get between seven and nine hours of sleep. Our body goes into dreaming mode when we enter REM sleep, which stands for Rapid Eye Movement. Your body cycles through a period of REM sleep every 90 minutes, and every time you enter this deep phase of sleep, you go deeper. So, the more REM cycles you can get, the deeper your sleep and the more vivid your dreams will be. If you do not get enough sleep, your body goes into REM less, and you will have fewer dreams, and dreams that are harder to remember.

One more note about preparing before bed: Beware of what you consume. Stay away from any drugs or pharmaceuticals before bed, including but not limited to alcohol, caffeine, sleep aids and other drugs that affect your memory or sleep. If you take these, they will alter your mind-state in your dreams, and you may have more difficulty remembering your dreams. Even light snacking can disrupt your body's systems and affect your sleep, especially if the items are high in sugar. It is best to stop eating at least two to three hours before bed.

Prepare Your Wake-Up Routine

The best way to wake up and remember your dreams in the morning is to have a peaceful and delicate alarm clock. You don't want an alarm clock that jars you awake with loud buzzing. It's also not best to have to run across the room to run it off. If you wake slowly, lying in bed, you have a better chance of holding onto the dream state you were just in.

If you can, set your alarm clock to a gentle sound to wake you, or have a roommate or partner gentle nudge you awake. Have a sign on your alarm clock or near your bed that asks you, "What did you dream?" (Or keep this journal close by!) If you keep this sign nearby, it will be the first thing you think when you wake up.

If you can, lay down (without falling asleep) and keep your eyes closed, picturing what you remember from your dream. Try to remember as much as you can. Sometimes it is easy to think that we can just get up and brush our teeth and start the coffee pot, and then we will focus on our dreams and write them down. But even if just a few minutes pass, you switch back into "reality" mode and your dreams easily get lost. So do your best to cultivate a habit of spending a few minutes in bed in the morning remembering your dreams.

Record What You Remember

Writing down your dream is the best way to save it for future reference. Just the act of writing down your dream will actually make you better and better at remembering it as time goes on. Some people who keep dream journals find that some mornings they are in such a trance-like state between the dreaming and waking world that they don't remember writing down their dreams in their journal! You will be amazed what it feels like to look at your handwriting and reading this story that seems so foreign. Often, though, once you begin reading your dream journal, you will once again see the images from your dream in your mind, and you may remember a few more details you had forgotten.

The dream journal sections of this book will guide you through what to remember and pay attention to in your dreams.

Those are just a few tips for better remembering your dreams, and how to set up the right environment to have more vivid dreams and remember them better. In the next chapter, we will look at the stages of sleep more in-depth.

3 THE STAGES OF SLEEP & DREAMING

IN THIS CHAPTER, YOU WILL learn about the stages of sleep and dreaming. Remember, even if you can't remember your dreams, if you are getting enough sleep (usually more than seven hours) and you are not using alcohol or drugs, you are dreaming, you just can't remember it.

Pre-REM Sleep

You may remember the stage of REM sleep from a previous chapter. It stand for Rapid Eye Movement. There are several different stages of REM sleep, but overall, it is in this stage that you dream. However, to get into that stage, you must first fall asleep. There are several sleep stages that come first.

The first stage of sleep lasts for five to 10 minutes, and is when you have just fallen asleep. It is easy to wake you during this stage, and if something does wake you, you may remember this stage as feeling just on the brink of sleep.

During the second stage, changes start to happen to your body. You body temperature begins to drop, and your heart rate slows in preparation for the next stage of pre-REM sleep.

The next stage is what people commonly refer to as a deep sleep. If someone woke you up during this stage, you would feel a bit "out of it" for a few minutes while you re-orientated to the waking world. In this deep stage of Non-REM sleep, more changes are happening in your body. Your body is repairing or growing your bones, muscle tissue, other tissues, and your immune system is growing stronger. This is why rest is imperative for the ill, and also why you need extra rest if you are doing a lot of exercise that is tearing your muscles.

Now that your body has gone through the Pre-REM stages, you are ready for dreaming.

REM Sleep

The Rapid Eye Movement stage of sleep begins about 90 minutes after you first fall into sleep. Surprisingly, it only lasts 10 minutes, and it is during this time that you dream. You heart rate may quicken, and your brain activity skyrockets. However, your muscles become paralyzed.

Once you exit REM sleep, you go back into the second stage of Pre-REM sleep, and then the third, and then REM sleep once more. These stages repeat over and over throughout the night, up to even five times. Each time you enter REM sleep, the stage becomes longer. During your last stage of REM sleep, you may be dreaming for up to an hour! That is why we need to rest for so long each night; we need to achieve that long REM period of sleep and dreaming.

Hopefully you understand a bit more about how your body gets you ready to dream during the night. In the next chapter, we will look at a bit of the history of dream interpretation.

4 HISTORY OF DREAM INTERPRETATION

FOR AS LONG AS HUMANS have been alive, we have dreamed. Across time, different cultures have taken different approaches to the dream life, and seen different meaning in its symbols and mysteries. Learning a bit about the history of dream interpretation can be illuminating to your own dream analysis practice.

Ancient Ideas

In ancient Egypt and Greece, dreams were seen as a supernatural message that was being communicated to humans from an outside force, or from God. Spiritual leaders were the only ones who could discern the meanings of dreams, and they were brought in to counsel people about what they had seen in their sleep. Dreams could foreshadow the future, cure sickness, or be direct messages from God.

The ancient Chinese also had an ancient book of dream interpretation in the vein of traditional Chinese medicine. They questioned how we knew whether we were in our waking life or our dream life, and saw dreams as an alternate reality.

In Christian literature, dreams are sometimes referred to as "visions," and Joseph was even mentioned in the Bible to be an interpreter of dreams.

Modern Approaches

It was in the late 19th century that dream interpretation came back into fashion with the help of psychoanalysis and famous psychologist Sigmund Freud. Freud said that dreams are a way to look into our souls and unconscious desires, beliefs and wishes. Freud said that dreams come from "day residue" or things that have happened or we have been concerned with from the day before. We aren't always conscious of what is troubling us, so when these things appear in our dreams as symbols, it becomes important to interpret them to understand our subconscious.

Scientific Understandings

There is a lot of research into the physical function of dreams, and they reveal that sleep and dreaming are a way to "reset" the human mind and body. As you learned in the last chapter, body tissues grow and repair during deep sleep, but it is also our brains that benefit from the rest. Have you ever tried to go through your normal day on little or no sleep, and found yourself making terrible decisions? We need adequate sleep to function properly, and scientists believe it is brain repair, and not just the physical body, that needs this nightly unconscious.

One scientific hypothesis states that dreaming is a method of storing our emotional memories. The brain strengthen some neural connections, but then cuts down others it deems unnecessary. After all, if you remembered everything from your days, you would be overwhelmed by all the unimportant details.

Today, some scientists are skeptical of dream interpretation. It is true that it does not have scientific backing, but that does not mean it cannot be useful for you. Any activity we undertake to better understand ourselves can provide us with greater insight, as long as we proceed with caution. So, in the next chapter, we will tell you the best way to interpret your dreams.

5 How to Interpret Your Dreams

In this chapter, you will learn how to interpret your dreams. We will go over several strategies and tell you everything you need to know about effectively understanding what your dreams actually mean.

Set Up the Right Environment

As mentioned in the chapter about how to better remember your dreams, setting up the right environment to analyze your dreams is important. The more you can capture and remember from your dream, the more insightful your analysis will be.

So remember to get a good night's rest unimpeded by drugs or alcohol, keep your dream journal or notepad next to your bed, and make an effort to remember your dream first thing when you wake up in the morning.

Starting a new habit is always hard, but once you get the hang of it, you will become better and better at remembering your dreams.

Write Down Everything You Can Remember

Guiding by our questions in the journal section of this book, you should record as much as you can remember from your dreams. Keep track of people, colors, situations, environment, thoughts you had in your dream, problems you had, and any more details. Do not try to create a story or narrative where there isn't one, however. Dreams are usually all over the place, and lack a central story or plot. This is perfectly normal, so just accept your dreams as they are, and do not try to make them "make sense" as though they were a movie.

Just record what you can remember as best to your ability, even if it seems strange. It is also a good idea to keep your dream journal private, so if you have an embarrassing or personal dream, you can record it without worry that someone will judge you for it. Remember, you are doing this for you, so be as honest with yourself as you can.

Look For Simple Explanations First

Did you have a dream where you bombed the job interview you have coming up next week? You don't need to look up the symbol for "job interview," as this dream is probably a very literal interpretation of how you are feeling. You are worried about the job interview, and so you had a very literal dream about failing that job interview. Do not feel as though you are not having interesting dreams if they are literal; this just means that you are very in-tune with your subconscious, and you are very aware of your own thoughts and feelings.

Also look for patterns that relate to recent conversations you have had, movies you have watched, or situations you have been in. You might have a dream about a bear because you watched a nature show about bears a few nights ago. Our mind may just be clearing out associations or trying to make sense of them while you sleep.

Dreams that have very straightforward meanings can be very useful to you in your waking life. For example, you can spend more time preparing for that job interview, and make sure to feel calm and collected the evening before, perhaps even thinking about acing the interview as you fall asleep. Dreams can help to show you how you are really feeling about a situation, and therefore illuminate your subconscious to you, even if in a literal way.

Then Look for Emotions & Symbols

Many times our dreams look nothing like our actual life, and so it is much harder to understand what they mean. But dream interpretation will help you figure out how you really feel, and perhaps you will learn something about yourself that you did not know!

The first step with more abstract dreams is to look for the dominant emotions from the dream. Whether happiness, anger, sadness, jealousy, fear, excitement or any other number of emotions, try to connect this to a real-life feeling you have. When was the last time you felt the dream emotion in your waking life? Does that situation have any other connections to the things you saw in your dream?

The next step is to look for the major symbols of your dream. What was the most memorable image that stays with you from your dream? Look up the symbol in the dream dictionary, and see if you can make any connections to real-life situations. Be sparing with using the dream dictionary, as your dream can quickly become confusing and you will have too many symbols to make sense of. Just choose one symbol to start, and see what situation in your waking life this symbol could be pointing to.

See the Patterns Over Time

As you get better at honing your dream interpretation skills and ability to remember your dreams, you will find that certain patterns start to emerge. You may realize that a lot of your dreams point to anxiety with work, or memories of a past relationship. Once you see these patterns, you will realize that something you were perhaps aware of about yourself, but didn't think was a big deal, has a lot more importance to you than you thought.

Maybe you knew work was stressful, but thought it was manageable. If you keep having dreams that point to work anxiety, it may be time to address this anxiety in the waking world. You can take steps to manage your stress, change something about your job, or find a new outlet for that stress. Maybe you thought you were over a past relationship, but your constant dreams tell you that you are not. You can do more investigation of your emotions in your waking life by talking to friends, journaling, or getting back into the dating world to meet someone new.

Dreams can really be illuminating this way, when you don't just see them night-by-night, but take them as larger patterns over weeks or months.

Be Honest With Yourself

Dream interpretation is all about you. There is no right or wrong way to do it, as well all have different dreams and different ways of deriving meaning from them. What is most important is that you approach dream interpretation with honesty to yourself and an open mind. You may learn some things that surprise you, or may be difficult to come to terms with. You cannot be afraid of really looking deeply within yourself to admit your fears, find out your true desires, and learn who you really are and want to become.

Interpreting your dreams will help you connect with yourself in ways you hadn't before, and it can change your life, if you are committed to just spending a few minutes each day to record your dreams and consider them.

I hope you have a great journey in interpreting your dreams, and before we get to the actual journal, we have one note about a type of dreaming you may have heard of — "lucid dreaming" — in the next chapter.

6 Lucid Dreaming

Before we get to the dream journaling section of this book, we wanted to share a bit about lucid dreaming, as you may be curious about it if you are interested in interpreting your dreams.

Lucid dreaming means that you are aware that you are in a dream while you are in it. It happens on occasion to most people, but there are some people who try to figure out how they can lucid dream every night, and gain greater control over their dreams. This is not for everyone, as it will take away some of the mystery of your dreams, and may hurt your dream interpretation.

However, even if you can control some aspects of your dreams, you will not always be able to control all of them, so you should still have plenty of symbols and scenarios to interpret the next day with dream analysis. Some lucid dreamers try to control every aspect of their dreams, but this is during advanced study. In the beginning stages of lucid dreaming, you will only be able to control yourself. Then, you learn how to control your environment, and then, you learn how to control who else appears in your dream, and so on and so forth.

In some cases, lucid dreaming has been used as a method to treat nightmares, as it can give more control over the dream to the person having them.

That is just a short introduction to lucid dreaming, so that you understand the term, as you will probably come across it if you find yourself interested in interpreting dreams and learning about the dreaming world. However, it is absolutely not necessary to practice it or learn more to gain greater control over understanding and interpreting your dreams. With that, let's get to the dream journal section of this book!

7 How to Use the Dream Journal

WELCOME TO THE JOURNAL SECTION of this book about dream interpretation. Before we begin, we have a few notes about the best way to use this journal so as to get the most out of it.

Ebook vs. Paperback Version

For the ebook version of this dream journal, you can answer these questions in a notebook every morning after you have just awoken. Record the particular of your dream on one page, and then on the next, write down some interpretations you see. One method to doing dream interpretation is to record the dream in the morning, and then do the analysis right before you go to bed. This may lead to common themes in your dreams over time.

If you want to order another paperback version of these pages you can re-order here: bit.ly/dreampages

DREAM REMEMBRANCE

Dream Name: _____   Date: _____

First words/biggest impressions that come to mind from this dream:

_____   _____   _____
_____   _____   _____
_____   _____   _____
_____   _____   _____

Dream Summary: _____

_____
_____
_____
_____
_____
_____
_____

Primary emotion in this dream: ☐ Happiness ☐ Sadness ☐ Fear
☐ Anxiety ☐ Strength ☐ Bravery ☐ Love ☐ Excitement ☐ Vulnerability
☐ _____   ☐ _____   ☐ _____

Sketch a scene or image from this dream:

DREAM INTERPRETATION

What does this dream make you think of from your waking life?

_____

_____

_____

When was the last time you felt the primary emotion(s) from your dream in your waking life?_____

_____

_____

Choose a few symbols to investigate in the dream dictionary or online:

SYMBOL   MEANING

_____   _____

_____   _____

_____   _____

What is your interpretation of the dream? (In words, pictures or symbols)

```



```

Have you had this dream before? ☐Yes ☐ No ☐ Do not know
                              ☐ Recurs often ☐ Recurs occasionally

Was this dream significant in meaning to you?
☐Very meaningful ☐Somewhat meaningful ☐Not at all meaningful

Are there any actions you will take based on this dream in your waking life?
1. _____
2. _____
3. _____

DREAM REMEMBRANCE

Dream Name: _____   Date: _____

First words/biggest impressions that come to mind from this dream:

_____   _____   _____

_____   _____   _____

_____   _____   _____

_____   _____   _____

Dream Summary: _____

_____

_____

_____

_____

_____

_____

_____

Primary emotion in this dream: ☐ Happiness ☐ Sadness ☐ Fear
☐ Anxiety ☐ Strength ☐ Bravery ☐ Love ☐ Excitement ☐ Vulnerability
☐ _____   ☐ _____   ☐ _____

Sketch a scene or image from this dream:

DREAM INTERPRETATION

What does this dream make you think of from your waking life?

_____

_____

_____

When was the last time you felt the primary emotion(s) from your dream in your waking life?_____

_____

_____

Choose a few symbols to investigate in the dream dictionary or online:

SYMBOL   MEANING

_____   _____

_____   _____

_____   _____

What is your interpretation of the dream? (In words, pictures or symbols)

```



```

Have you had this dream before? ☐Yes ☐ No ☐ Do not know
                                    ☐ Recurs often ☐ Recurs occasionally

Was this dream significant in meaning to you?
☐Very meaningful ☐Somewhat meaningful ☐Not at all meaningful

Are there any actions you will take based on this dream in your waking life?

1. _____

2. _____

3. _____

DREAM REMEMBRANCE

Dream Name: _____   Date: _____

First words/biggest impressions that come to mind from this dream:

_____   _____   _____

_____   _____   _____

_____   _____   _____

_____   _____   _____

Dream Summary: _____

_____

_____

_____

_____

_____

_____

_____

Primary emotion in this dream: ☐ Happiness ☐ Sadness ☐ Fear
☐ Anxiety ☐ Strength ☐ Bravery ☐ Love ☐ Excitement ☐ Vulnerability
☐ _____   ☐ _____   ☐ _____

Sketch a scene or image from this dream:

DREAM INTERPRETATION

What does this dream make you think of from your waking life?

_____
_____
_____

When was the last time you felt the primary emotion(s) from your dream in your waking life?_____

_____
_____

Choose a few symbols to investigate in the dream dictionary or online:

SYMBOL   MEANING

_____   _____
_____   _____
_____   _____

What is your interpretation of the dream? (In words, pictures or symbols)

```
┌─────────────────────────────────────────┐
│                                           │
│                                           │
│                                           │
│                                           │
│                                           │
└─────────────────────────────────────────┘
```

Have you had this dream before? ☐ Yes ☐ No ☐ Do not know
☐ Recurs often ☐ Recurs occasionally

Was this dream significant in meaning to you?
☐ Very meaningful ☐ Somewhat meaningful ☐ Not at all meaningful

Are there any actions you will take based on this dream in your waking life?

1. _____
2. _____
3. _____

DREAM REMEMBRANCE

Dream Name: _____   Date: _____

First words/biggest impressions that come to mind from this dream:

_____   _____   _____

_____   _____   _____

_____   _____   _____

_____   _____   _____

Dream Summary: _____

_____

_____

_____

_____

_____

_____

_____

Primary emotion in this dream: ☐ Happiness ☐ Sadness ☐ Fear
☐ Anxiety ☐ Strength ☐ Bravery ☐ Love ☐ Excitement ☐ Vulnerability
☐ _____   ☐ _____   ☐ _____

Sketch a scene or image from this dream:

DREAM INTERPRETATION

What does this dream make you think of from your waking life?

_____

_____

_____

When was the last time you felt the primary emotion(s) from your dream in your waking life?_____

_____

_____

Choose a few symbols to investigate in the dream dictionary or online:

SYMBOL   MEANING

_____   _____

_____   _____

_____   _____

What is your interpretation of the dream? (In words, pictures or symbols)

Have you had this dream before? ☐Yes ☐ No ☐ Do not know
☐ Recurs often ☐ Recurs occasionally

Was this dream significant in meaning to you?
☐Very meaningful ☐Somewhat meaningful ☐Not at all meaningful

Are there any actions you will take based on this dream in your waking life?
1. _____
2. _____
3. _____

DREAM REMEMBRANCE

Dream Name: _____   Date: _____

First words/biggest impressions that come to mind from this dream:

_____   _____   _____

_____   _____   _____

_____   _____   _____

_____   _____   _____

Dream Summary: _____

_____

_____

_____

_____

_____

_____

_____

Primary emotion in this dream: ☐ Happiness ☐ Sadness ☐ Fear
☐ Anxiety ☐ Strength ☐ Bravery ☐ Love ☐ Excitement ☐ Vulnerability
☐ _____   ☐ _____   ☐ _____

Sketch a scene or image from this dream:

_____

DREAM INTERPRETATION

What does this dream make you think of from your waking life?

_____

_____

_____

When was the last time you felt the primary emotion(s) from your dream in your waking life?_____

_____

_____

Choose a few symbols to investigate in the dream dictionary or online:

SYMBOL   MEANING

_____   _____

_____   _____

_____   _____

What is your interpretation of the dream? (In words, pictures or symbols)

+---+
| |
| |
| |
| |
| |
+---+

Have you had this dream before? ☐Yes ☐ No ☐ Do not know

☐ Recurs often ☐ Recurs occasionally

Was this dream significant in meaning to you?
☐Very meaningful ☐Somewhat meaningful ☐Not at all meaningful

Are there any actions you will take based on this dream in your waking life?

1._____

2._____

3._____

DREAM REMEMBRANCE

Dream Name: _____   Date: _____

First words/biggest impressions that come to mind from this dream:

_____   _____   _____
_____   _____   _____
_____   _____   _____
_____   _____   _____

Dream Summary: _____
_____
_____
_____
_____
_____
_____
_____

Primary emotion in this dream: ☐ Happiness ☐ Sadness ☐ Fear
☐ Anxiety ☐ Strength ☐ Bravery ☐ Love ☐ Excitement ☐ Vulnerability
☐ _____ ☐ _____ ☐ _____

Sketch a scene or image from this dream:

DREAM INTERPRETATION

What does this dream make you think of from your waking life?

_____

_____

_____

When was the last time you felt the primary emotion(s) from your dream in your waking life?_____

_____

_____

Choose a few symbols to investigate in the dream dictionary or online:

SYMBOL   MEANING

_____   _____

_____   _____

_____   _____

What is your interpretation of the dream? (In words, pictures or symbols)

Have you had this dream before? ☐ Yes ☐ No ☐ Do not know
☐ Recurs often ☐ Recurs occasionally

Was this dream significant in meaning to you?
☐ Very meaningful ☐ Somewhat meaningful ☐ Not at all meaningful

Are there any actions you will take based on this dream in your waking life?

1. _____
2. _____
3. _____

DREAM REMEMBRANCE

Dream Name: _____   Date: _____

First words/biggest impressions that come to mind from this dream:

_____   _____   _____

_____   _____   _____

_____   _____   _____

_____   _____   _____

Dream Summary: _____

_____

_____

_____

_____

_____

_____

_____

Primary emotion in this dream: ☐ Happiness ☐ Sadness ☐ Fear
☐ Anxiety ☐ Strength ☐ Bravery ☐ Love ☐ Excitement ☐ Vulnerability
☐ _____   ☐ _____   ☐ _____

Sketch a scene or image from this dream:

DREAM INTERPRETATION

What does this dream make you think of from your waking life?

_____
_____
_____

When was the last time you felt the primary emotion(s) from your dream in your waking life?_____

_____
_____

Choose a few symbols to investigate in the dream dictionary or online:

SYMBOL   MEANING

_____   _____
_____   _____
_____   _____

What is your interpretation of the dream? (In words, pictures or symbols)

Have you had this dream before? ☐Yes ☐ No ☐ Do not know
                              ☐ Recurs often ☐ Recurs occasionally

Was this dream significant in meaning to you?
☐Very meaningful ☐Somewhat meaningful ☐Not at all meaningful

Are there any actions you will take based on this dream in your waking life?
1. _____
2. _____
3. _____

DREAM REMEMBRANCE

Dream Name: _____   Date: _____

First words/biggest impressions that come to mind from this dream:

_____   _____   _____

_____   _____   _____

_____   _____   _____

_____   _____   _____

Dream Summary: _____

_____

_____

_____

_____

_____

_____

_____

Primary emotion in this dream: ☐ Happiness ☐ Sadness ☐ Fear
☐ Anxiety ☐ Strength ☐ Bravery ☐ Love ☐ Excitement ☐ Vulnerability
☐ _____   ☐ _____   ☐ _____

Sketch a scene or image from this dream:

DREAM INTERPRETATION

What does this dream make you think of from your waking life?

_____
_____
_____

When was the last time you felt the primary emotion(s) from your dream in your waking life?_____

_____
_____

Choose a few symbols to investigate in the dream dictionary or online:

SYMBOL   MEANING

_____   _____
_____   _____
_____   _____

What is your interpretation of the dream? (In words, pictures or symbols)

```




```

Have you had this dream before? ☐Yes ☐ No ☐ Do not know
                                   ☐ Recurs often ☐ Recurs occasionally

Was this dream significant in meaning to you?
☐Very meaningful ☐Somewhat meaningful ☐Not at all meaningful

Are there any actions you will take based on this dream in your waking life?
   1. _____
   2. _____
   3. _____

DREAM REMEMBRANCE

Dream Name: _____   Date: _____

First words/biggest impressions that come to mind from this dream:

_____   _____   _____
_____   _____   _____
_____   _____   _____
_____   _____   _____

Dream Summary: _____

_____
_____
_____
_____
_____
_____
_____

Primary emotion in this dream: ☐ Happiness ☐ Sadness ☐ Fear
☐ Anxiety ☐ Strength ☐ Bravery ☐ Love ☐ Excitement ☐ Vulnerability
☐ _____   ☐ _____   ☐ _____

Sketch a scene or image from this dream:

DREAM INTERPRETATION

What does this dream make you think of from your waking life?

_____

_____

_____

When was the last time you felt the primary emotion(s) from your dream in your waking life?_____

_____

_____

Choose a few symbols to investigate in the dream dictionary or online:

SYMBOL   MEANING

_____   _____

_____   _____

_____   _____

What is your interpretation of the dream? (In words, pictures or symbols)

```
┌─────────────────────────────────────────────────┐
│                                                 │
│                                                 │
│                                                 │
│                                                 │
│                                                 │
└─────────────────────────────────────────────────┘
```

Have you had this dream before? ☐Yes ☐ No ☐ Do not know
☐ Recurs often ☐ Recurs occasionally

Was this dream significant in meaning to you?
☐Very meaningful ☐Somewhat meaningful ☐Not at all meaningful

Are there any actions you will take based on this dream in your waking life?
1. _____
2. _____
3. _____

DREAM REMEMBRANCE

Dream Name: _____   Date: _____

First words/biggest impressions that come to mind from this dream:

_____   _____   _____

_____   _____   _____

_____   _____   _____

_____   _____   _____

Dream Summary: _____

_____

_____

_____

_____

_____

_____

_____

Primary emotion in this dream: ☐ Happiness ☐ Sadness ☐ Fear
☐ Anxiety ☐ Strength ☐ Bravery ☐ Love ☐ Excitement ☐ Vulnerability
☐ _____   ☐ _____   ☐ _____

Sketch a scene or image from this dream:

DREAM INTERPRETATION

What does this dream make you think of from your waking life?

_____

_____

_____

When was the last time you felt the primary emotion(s) from your dream in your waking life?_____

_____

_____

Choose a few symbols to investigate in the dream dictionary or online:

SYMBOL   MEANING

_____   _____

_____   _____

_____   _____

What is your interpretation of the dream? (In words, pictures or symbols)

Have you had this dream before? ☐Yes ☐ No ☐ Do not know

☐ Recurs often ☐ Recurs occasionally

Was this dream significant in meaning to you?
☐Very meaningful ☐Somewhat meaningful ☐Not at all meaningful

Are there any actions you will take based on this dream in your waking life?

1. _____
2. _____
3. _____

DREAM REMEMBRANCE

Dream Name: _____   Date: _____

First words/biggest impressions that come to mind from this dream:

_____   _____   _____
_____   _____   _____
_____   _____   _____
_____   _____   _____

Dream Summary: _____
_____
_____
_____
_____
_____
_____
_____

Primary emotion in this dream: ☐ Happiness ☐ Sadness ☐ Fear
☐ Anxiety ☐ Strength ☐ Bravery ☐ Love ☐ Excitement ☐ Vulnerability
☐ _____   ☐ _____   ☐ _____

Sketch a scene or image from this dream:

DREAM INTERPRETATION

What does this dream make you think of from your waking life?

_____

_____

_____

When was the last time you felt the primary emotion(s) from your dream in your waking life?_____

_____

_____

Choose a few symbols to investigate in the dream dictionary or online:

SYMBOL   MEANING

_____   _____

_____   _____

_____   _____

What is your interpretation of the dream? (In words, pictures or symbols)

Have you had this dream before? ☐Yes ☐ No ☐ Do not know

☐ Recurs often ☐ Recurs occasionally

Was this dream significant in meaning to you?

☐Very meaningful ☐Somewhat meaningful ☐Not at all meaningful

Are there any actions you will take based on this dream in your waking life?

1. _____

2. _____

3. _____

DREAM REMEMBRANCE

Dream Name: _____   Date: _____

First words/biggest impressions that come to mind from this dream:

_____   _____   _____
_____   _____   _____
_____   _____   _____
_____   _____   _____

Dream Summary: _____

_____
_____
_____
_____
_____
_____
_____

Primary emotion in this dream: ☐ Happiness ☐ Sadness ☐ Fear
☐ Anxiety ☐ Strength ☐ Bravery ☐ Love ☐ Excitement ☐ Vulnerability
☐ _____   ☐ _____   ☐ _____

Sketch a scene or image from this dream:

DREAM INTERPRETATION

What does this dream make you think of from your waking life?

_____

_____

_____

When was the last time you felt the primary emotion(s) from your dream in your waking life?_____

_____

_____

Choose a few symbols to investigate in the dream dictionary or online:

SYMBOL   MEANING

_____   _____

_____   _____

_____   _____

What is your interpretation of the dream? (In words, pictures or symbols)

```



```

Have you had this dream before? ☐Yes ☐ No ☐ Do not know
☐ Recurs often ☐ Recurs occasionally

Was this dream significant in meaning to you?
☐Very meaningful ☐Somewhat meaningful ☐Not at all meaningful

Are there any actions you will take based on this dream in your waking life?
1. _____
2. _____
3. _____

DREAM REMEMBRANCE

Dream Name: _____   Date: _____

First words/biggest impressions that come to mind from this dream:

_____   _____   _____

_____   _____   _____

_____   _____   _____

_____   _____   _____

Dream Summary: _____

_____

_____

_____

_____

_____

_____

_____

Primary emotion in this dream: ☐ Happiness ☐ Sadness ☐ Fear
☐ Anxiety ☐ Strength ☐ Bravery ☐ Love ☐ Excitement ☐ Vulnerability
☐ _____ ☐ _____ ☐ _____

Sketch a scene or image from this dream:

40

DREAM INTERPRETATION

What does this dream make you think of from your waking life?

_____

_____

_____

When was the last time you felt the primary emotion(s) from your dream in your waking life?_____

_____

_____

Choose a few symbols to investigate in the dream dictionary or online:

SYMBOL   MEANING

_____   _____

_____   _____

_____   _____

What is your interpretation of the dream? (In words, pictures or symbols)

Have you had this dream before? ☐ Yes ☐ No ☐ Do not know
☐ Recurs often ☐ Recurs occasionally

Was this dream significant in meaning to you?
☐ Very meaningful ☐ Somewhat meaningful ☐ Not at all meaningful

Are there any actions you will take based on this dream in your waking life?
1. _____
2. _____
3. _____

DREAM REMEMBRANCE

Dream Name: _____   Date: _____

First words/biggest impressions that come to mind from this dream:

_____   _____   _____

_____   _____   _____

_____   _____   _____

_____   _____   _____

Dream Summary: _____

_____

_____

_____

_____

_____

_____

_____

Primary emotion in this dream: ☐ Happiness ☐ Sadness ☐ Fear
☐ Anxiety ☐ Strength ☐ Bravery ☐ Love ☐ Excitement ☐ Vulnerability
☐ _____   ☐ _____   ☐ _____

Sketch a scene or image from this dream:

DREAM INTERPRETATION

What does this dream make you think of from your waking life?

_____

_____

_____

When was the last time you felt the primary emotion(s) from your dream in your waking life?_____

_____

_____

Choose a few symbols to investigate in the dream dictionary or online:

SYMBOL   MEANING

_____   _____

_____   _____

_____   _____

What is your interpretation of the dream? (In words, pictures or symbols)

Have you had this dream before? ☐ Yes ☐ No ☐ Do not know
                                                ☐ Recurs often ☐ Recurs occasionally

Was this dream significant in meaning to you?
☐ Very meaningful ☐ Somewhat meaningful ☐ Not at all meaningful

Are there any actions you will take based on this dream in your waking life?
1. _____
2. _____
3. _____

DREAM REMEMBRANCE

Dream Name: _____   Date: _____

First words/biggest impressions that come to mind from this dream:

_____   _____   _____
_____   _____   _____
_____   _____   _____
_____   _____   _____

Dream Summary: _____

_____
_____
_____
_____
_____
_____
_____

Primary emotion in this dream: ☐ Happiness ☐ Sadness ☐ Fear
☐ Anxiety ☐ Strength ☐ Bravery ☐ Love ☐ Excitement ☐ Vulnerability
☐ _____   ☐ _____   ☐ _____

Sketch a scene or image from this dream:

DREAM INTERPRETATION

What does this dream make you think of from your waking life?

_____

_____

_____

When was the last time you felt the primary emotion(s) from your dream in your waking life?_____

_____

_____

Choose a few symbols to investigate in the dream dictionary or online:

SYMBOL   MEANING

_____   _____

_____   _____

_____   _____

What is your interpretation of the dream? (In words, pictures or symbols)

```



```

Have you had this dream before? ☐ Yes ☐ No ☐ Do not know

☐ Recurs often ☐ Recurs occasionally

Was this dream significant in meaning to you?
☐ Very meaningful ☐ Somewhat meaningful ☐ Not at all meaningful

Are there any actions you will take based on this dream in your waking life?

1. _____

2. _____

3. _____

DREAM REMEMBRANCE

Dream Name: _____ Date: _____

First words/biggest impressions that come to mind from this dream:

_____   _____   _____
_____   _____   _____
_____   _____   _____
_____   _____   _____

Dream Summary: _____

_____
_____
_____
_____
_____
_____
_____

Primary emotion in this dream: ☐ Happiness ☐ Sadness ☐ Fear
☐ Anxiety ☐ Strength ☐ Bravery ☐ Love ☐ Excitement ☐ Vulnerability
☐ _____   ☐ _____   ☐ _____

Sketch a scene or image from this dream:

DREAM INTERPRETATION

What does this dream make you think of from your waking life?

_____

_____

_____

When was the last time you felt the primary emotion(s) from your dream in your waking life?_____

_____

_____

Choose a few symbols to investigate in the dream dictionary or online:

SYMBOL   MEANING

_____   _____

_____   _____

_____   _____

What is your interpretation of the dream? (In words, pictures or symbols)

Have you had this dream before? ☐ Yes ☐ No ☐ Do not know
                                    ☐ Recurs often ☐ Recurs occasionally

Was this dream significant in meaning to you?
☐ Very meaningful ☐ Somewhat meaningful ☐ Not at all meaningful

Are there any actions you will take based on this dream in your waking life?
1. _____
2. _____
3. _____

DREAM REMEMBRANCE

Dream Name: _____   Date: _____

First words/biggest impressions that come to mind from this dream:

_____   _____   _____
_____   _____   _____
_____   _____   _____
_____   _____   _____

Dream Summary: _____
_____
_____
_____
_____
_____
_____
_____

Primary emotion in this dream: ☐ Happiness ☐ Sadness ☐ Fear
☐ Anxiety ☐ Strength ☐ Bravery ☐ Love ☐ Excitement ☐ Vulnerability
☐ _____   ☐ _____   ☐ _____

Sketch a scene or image from this dream:

DREAM INTERPRETATION

What does this dream make you think of from your waking life?

_____

_____

_____

When was the last time you felt the primary emotion(s) from your dream in your waking life?_____

_____

_____

Choose a few symbols to investigate in the dream dictionary or online:

SYMBOL   MEANING

_____   _____

_____   _____

_____   _____

What is your interpretation of the dream? (In words, pictures or symbols)

```




```

Have you had this dream before? ☐Yes ☐ No ☐ Do not know
                                ☐ Recurs often ☐ Recurs occasionally

Was this dream significant in meaning to you?
☐Very meaningful ☐Somewhat meaningful ☐Not at all meaningful

Are there any actions you will take based on this dream in your waking life?
1. _____
2. _____
3. _____

DREAM REMEMBRANCE

Dream Name: _____   Date: _____

First words/biggest impressions that come to mind from this dream:

_____   _____   _____

_____   _____   _____

_____   _____   _____

_____   _____   _____

Dream Summary: _____

_____

_____

_____

_____

_____

_____

_____

Primary emotion in this dream: ☐ Happiness ☐ Sadness ☐ Fear
☐ Anxiety ☐ Strength ☐ Bravery ☐ Love ☐ Excitement ☐ Vulnerability
☐ _____   ☐ _____   ☐ _____

Sketch a scene or image from this dream:

DREAM INTERPRETATION

What does this dream make you think of from your waking life?

_____

_____

_____

When was the last time you felt the primary emotion(s) from your dream in your waking life?_____

_____

_____

Choose a few symbols to investigate in the dream dictionary or online:

SYMBOL   MEANING

_____   _____

_____   _____

_____   _____

What is your interpretation of the dream? (In words, pictures or symbols)

What is your interpretation of the dream? (In words, pictures or symbols)

Have you had this dream before? ☐ Yes ☐ No ☐ Do not know
                                 ☐ Recurs often ☐ Recurs occasionally

Was this dream significant in meaning to you?
☐ Very meaningful ☐ Somewhat meaningful ☐ Not at all meaningful

Are there any actions you will take based on this dream in your waking life?
1. _____
2. _____
3. _____

DREAM REMEMBRANCE

Dream Name: _____   Date: _____

First words/biggest impressions that come to mind from this dream:

_____   _____   _____

_____   _____   _____

_____   _____   _____

_____   _____   _____

Dream Summary: _____

_____

_____

_____

_____

_____

_____

_____

Primary emotion in this dream: ☐ Happiness ☐ Sadness ☐ Fear
☐ Anxiety ☐ Strength ☐ Bravery ☐ Love ☐ Excitement ☐ Vulnerability
☐ _____   ☐ _____   ☐ _____

Sketch a scene or image from this dream:

DREAM INTERPRETATION

What does this dream make you think of from your waking life?

_____
_____
_____

When was the last time you felt the primary emotion(s) from your dream in your waking life?_____

_____
_____

Choose a few symbols to investigate in the dream dictionary or online:

SYMBOL   MEANING

_____   _____
_____   _____
_____   _____

What is your interpretation of the dream? (In words, pictures or symbols)

```



```

Have you had this dream before? ☐ Yes ☐ No ☐ Do not know
                                ☐ Recurs often ☐ Recurs occasionally

Was this dream significant in meaning to you?
☐ Very meaningful ☐ Somewhat meaningful ☐ Not at all meaningful

Are there any actions you will take based on this dream in your waking life?
   1. _____
   2. _____
   3. _____

DREAM REMEMBRANCE

Dream Name: _____   Date: _____

First words/biggest impressions that come to mind from this dream:

_____   _____   _____

_____   _____   _____

_____   _____   _____

_____   _____   _____

Dream Summary: _____

_____

_____

_____

_____

_____

_____

_____

Primary emotion in this dream: ☐ Happiness ☐ Sadness ☐ Fear
☐ Anxiety ☐ Strength ☐ Bravery ☐ Love ☐ Excitement ☐ Vulnerability
☐ _____   ☐ _____   ☐ _____

Sketch a scene or image from this dream:

DREAM INTERPRETATION

What does this dream make you think of from your waking life?

_____
_____
_____

When was the last time you felt the primary emotion(s) from your dream in your waking life?_____
_____
_____

Choose a few symbols to investigate in the dream dictionary or online:

SYMBOL   MEANING

_____   _____
_____   _____
_____   _____

What is your interpretation of the dream? (In words, pictures or symbols)

Have you had this dream before? ☐ Yes ☐ No ☐ Do not know
                                ☐ Recurs often ☐ Recurs occasionally

Was this dream significant in meaning to you?
☐ Very meaningful ☐ Somewhat meaningful ☐ Not at all meaningful

Are there any actions you will take based on this dream in your waking life?
1. _____
2. _____
3. _____

DREAM REMEMBRANCE

Dream Name: _____   Date: _____

First words/biggest impressions that come to mind from this dream:

_____   _____   _____

_____   _____   _____

_____   _____   _____

_____   _____   _____

Dream Summary: _____

_____

_____

_____

_____

_____

_____

_____

Primary emotion in this dream: ☐ Happiness ☐ Sadness ☐ Fear
☐ Anxiety ☐ Strength ☐ Bravery ☐ Love ☐ Excitement ☐ Vulnerability
☐ _____   ☐ _____   ☐ _____

Sketch a scene or image from this dream:

DREAM INTERPRETATION

What does this dream make you think of from your waking life?

_____

_____

_____

When was the last time you felt the primary emotion(s) from your dream in your waking life?_____

_____

_____

Choose a few symbols to investigate in the dream dictionary or online:

SYMBOL   MEANING

_____   _____

_____   _____

_____   _____

What is your interpretation of the dream? (In words, pictures or symbols)

Have you had this dream before? ☐ Yes ☐ No ☐ Do not know
                               ☐ Recurs often ☐ Recurs occasionally

Was this dream significant in meaning to you?
☐ Very meaningful ☐ Somewhat meaningful ☐ Not at all meaningful

Are there any actions you will take based on this dream in your waking life?

1. _____
2. _____
3. _____

DREAM REMEMBRANCE

Dream Name: _____   Date: _____

First words/biggest impressions that come to mind from this dream:

_____   _____   _____

_____   _____   _____

_____   _____   _____

_____   _____   _____

Dream Summary: _____

_____

_____

_____

_____

_____

_____

_____

Primary emotion in this dream: ☐ Happiness ☐ Sadness ☐ Fear
☐ Anxiety ☐ Strength ☐ Bravery ☐ Love ☐ Excitement ☐ Vulnerability
☐ _____   ☐ _____   ☐ _____

Sketch a scene or image from this dream:

DREAM INTERPRETATION

What does this dream make you think of from your waking life?

_____

_____

_____

When was the last time you felt the primary emotion(s) from your dream in your waking life?_____

_____

_____

Choose a few symbols to investigate in the dream dictionary or online:

SYMBOL   MEANING

_____   _____

_____   _____

_____   _____

What is your interpretation of the dream? (In words, pictures or symbols)

Have you had this dream before? ☐Yes ☐ No ☐ Do not know

☐ Recurs often ☐ Recurs occasionally

Was this dream significant in meaning to you?

☐Very meaningful ☐Somewhat meaningful ☐Not at all meaningful

Are there any actions you will take based on this dream in your waking life?

1. _____

2. _____

3. _____

DREAM REMEMBRANCE

Dream Name: _____   Date: _____

First words/biggest impressions that come to mind from this dream:

_____   _____   _____

_____   _____   _____

_____   _____   _____

_____   _____   _____

Dream Summary: _____

_____

_____

_____

_____

_____

_____

_____

Primary emotion in this dream: ☐ Happiness ☐ Sadness ☐ Fear
☐ Anxiety ☐ Strength ☐ Bravery ☐ Love ☐ Excitement ☐ Vulnerability
☐ _____   ☐ _____   ☐ _____

Sketch a scene or image from this dream:

DREAM INTERPRETATION

What does this dream make you think of from your waking life?

_____
_____
_____

When was the last time you felt the primary emotion(s) from your dream in your waking life?_____
_____
_____

Choose a few symbols to investigate in the dream dictionary or online:

SYMBOL   MEANING

_____   _____
_____   _____
_____   _____

What is your interpretation of the dream? (In words, pictures or symbols)

Have you had this dream before? ☐Yes ☐ No ☐ Do not know
                                            ☐ Recurs often ☐ Recurs occasionally

Was this dream significant in meaning to you?
☐Very meaningful ☐Somewhat meaningful ☐Not at all meaningful

Are there any actions you will take based on this dream in your waking life?
1. _____
2. _____
3. _____

DREAM REMEMBRANCE

Dream Name: _____   Date: _____

First words/biggest impressions that come to mind from this dream:

_____   _____   _____

_____   _____   _____

_____   _____   _____

_____   _____   _____

Dream Summary: _____

_____

_____

_____

_____

_____

_____

_____

Primary emotion in this dream: ☐ Happiness ☐ Sadness ☐ Fear
☐ Anxiety ☐ Strength ☐ Bravery ☐ Love ☐ Excitement ☐ Vulnerability
☐ _____   ☐ _____   ☐ _____

Sketch a scene or image from this dream:

DREAM INTERPRETATION

What does this dream make you think of from your waking life?

_____

_____

_____

When was the last time you felt the primary emotion(s) from your dream in your waking life?_____

_____

_____

Choose a few symbols to investigate in the dream dictionary or online:

SYMBOL   MEANING

_____   _____

_____   _____

_____   _____

What is your interpretation of the dream? (In words, pictures or symbols)

```
┌─────────────────────────────────────────────┐
│                                             │
│                                             │
│                                             │
│                                             │
│                                             │
└─────────────────────────────────────────────┘
```

Have you had this dream before? ☐ Yes ☐ No ☐ Do not know
                              ☐ Recurs often ☐ Recurs occasionally

Was this dream significant in meaning to you?
☐ Very meaningful ☐ Somewhat meaningful ☐ Not at all meaningful

Are there any actions you will take based on this dream in your waking life?

1. _____

2. _____

3. _____

DREAM REMEMBRANCE

Dream Name: _____   Date: _____

First words/biggest impressions that come to mind from this dream:

_____   _____   _____

_____   _____   _____

_____   _____   _____

_____   _____   _____

Dream Summary: _____

_____

_____

_____

_____

_____

_____

_____

Primary emotion in this dream: ☐ Happiness ☐ Sadness ☐ Fear
☐ Anxiety ☐ Strength ☐ Bravery ☐ Love ☐ Excitement ☐ Vulnerability
☐ _____   ☐ _____   ☐ _____

Sketch a scene or image from this dream:

DREAM INTERPRETATION

What does this dream make you think of from your waking life?

_____

_____

_____

When was the last time you felt the primary emotion(s) from your dream in your waking life?_____

_____

_____

Choose a few symbols to investigate in the dream dictionary or online:

SYMBOL   MEANING

_____   _____

_____   _____

_____   _____

What is your interpretation of the dream? (In words, pictures or symbols)

```
[                                                        ]
[                                                        ]
[                                                        ]
[                                                        ]
```

Have you had this dream before? ☐Yes ☐ No ☐ Do not know
                                        ☐ Recurs often ☐ Recurs occasionally

Was this dream significant in meaning to you?
☐Very meaningful ☐Somewhat meaningful ☐Not at all meaningful

Are there any actions you will take based on this dream in your waking life?
    1. _____
    2. _____
    3. _____

DREAM REMEMBRANCE

Dream Name: _____   Date: _____

First words/biggest impressions that come to mind from this dream:

_____   _____   _____

_____   _____   _____

_____   _____   _____

_____   _____   _____

Dream Summary: _____

_____

_____

_____

_____

_____

_____

_____

Primary emotion in this dream: ☐ Happiness ☐ Sadness ☐ Fear
☐ Anxiety ☐ Strength ☐ Bravery ☐ Love ☐ Excitement ☐ Vulnerability
☐ _____   ☐ _____   ☐ _____

Sketch a scene or image from this dream:

DREAM INTERPRETATION

What does this dream make you think of from your waking life?

_____
_____
_____

When was the last time you felt the primary emotion(s) from your dream in your waking life?_____

_____
_____

Choose a few symbols to investigate in the dream dictionary or online:

SYMBOL   MEANING

_____   _____
_____   _____
_____   _____

What is your interpretation of the dream? (In words, pictures or symbols)

```



```

Have you had this dream before? ☐Yes ☐ No ☐ Do not know
                        ☐ Recurs often ☐ Recurs occasionally

Was this dream significant in meaning to you?
☐Very meaningful ☐Somewhat meaningful ☐Not at all meaningful

Are there any actions you will take based on this dream in your waking life?
1. _____
2. _____
3. _____

DREAM REMEMBRANCE

Dream Name: _____   Date: _____

First words/biggest impressions that come to mind from this dream:

_____   _____   _____

_____   _____   _____

_____   _____   _____

_____   _____   _____

Dream Summary: _____

_____

_____

_____

_____

_____

_____

_____

Primary emotion in this dream: ☐ Happiness ☐ Sadness ☐ Fear
☐ Anxiety ☐ Strength ☐ Bravery ☐ Love ☐ Excitement ☐ Vulnerability
☐ _____   ☐ _____   ☐ _____

Sketch a scene or image from this dream:

DREAM INTERPRETATION

What does this dream make you think of from your waking life?

_____
_____
_____

When was the last time you felt the primary emotion(s) from your dream in your waking life?_____

_____
_____

Choose a few symbols to investigate in the dream dictionary or online:

SYMBOL   MEANING

_____   _____

_____   _____

_____   _____

What is your interpretation of the dream? (In words, pictures or symbols)

```
[                                                        ]
[                                                        ]
[                                                        ]
[                                                        ]
[                                                        ]
```

Have you had this dream before? ☐Yes ☐ No ☐ Do not know

☐ Recurs often ☐ Recurs occasionally

Was this dream significant in meaning to you?
☐Very meaningful ☐Somewhat meaningful ☐Not at all meaningful

Are there any actions you will take based on this dream in your waking life?

1. _____

2. _____

3. _____

DREAM REMEMBRANCE

Dream Name: _____   Date: _____

First words/biggest impressions that come to mind from this dream:

_____   _____   _____
_____   _____   _____
_____   _____   _____
_____   _____   _____

Dream Summary: _____
_____
_____
_____
_____
_____
_____
_____

Primary emotion in this dream: ☐ Happiness ☐ Sadness ☐ Fear
☐ Anxiety ☐ Strength ☐ Bravery ☐ Love ☐ Excitement ☐ Vulnerability
☐ _____   ☐ _____   ☐ _____

Sketch a scene or image from this dream:

DREAM INTERPRETATION

What does this dream make you think of from your waking life?

_____

_____

_____

When was the last time you felt the primary emotion(s) from your dream in your waking life?_____

_____

_____

Choose a few symbols to investigate in the dream dictionary or online:

SYMBOL   MEANING

_____   _____

_____   _____

_____   _____

What is your interpretation of the dream? (In words, pictures or symbols)

Have you had this dream before? ☐Yes ☐ No ☐ Do not know

☐ Recurs often ☐ Recurs occasionally

Was this dream significant in meaning to you?

☐Very meaningful ☐Somewhat meaningful ☐Not at all meaningful

Are there any actions you will take based on this dream in your waking life?

1. _____

2. _____

3. _____

DREAM REMEMBRANCE

Dream Name: _____   Date: _____

First words/biggest impressions that come to mind from this dream:

_____   _____   _____

_____   _____   _____

_____   _____   _____

_____   _____   _____

Dream Summary: _____

_____

_____

_____

_____

_____

_____

_____

_____

Primary emotion in this dream: ☐ Happiness ☐ Sadness ☐ Fear
☐ Anxiety ☐ Strength ☐ Bravery ☐ Love ☐ Excitement ☐ Vulnerability
☐ _____   ☐ _____   ☐ _____

Sketch a scene or image from this dream:

DREAM INTERPRETATION

What does this dream make you think of from your waking life?

_____

_____

_____

When was the last time you felt the primary emotion(s) from your dream in your waking life?_____

_____

_____

Choose a few symbols to investigate in the dream dictionary or online:

SYMBOL   MEANING

_____   _____

_____   _____

_____   _____

What is your interpretation of the dream? (In words, pictures or symbols)

Have you had this dream before? ☐Yes ☐ No ☐ Do not know
☐ Recurs often ☐ Recurs occasionally

Was this dream significant in meaning to you?
☐Very meaningful ☐Somewhat meaningful ☐Not at all meaningful

Are there any actions you will take based on this dream in your waking life?

1. _____
2. _____
3. _____

DREAM REMEMBRANCE

Dream Name: _____   Date: _____

First words/biggest impressions that come to mind from this dream:

_____   _____   _____
_____   _____   _____
_____   _____   _____
_____   _____   _____

Dream Summary: _____
_____
_____
_____
_____
_____
_____
_____

Primary emotion in this dream: ☐ Happiness ☐ Sadness ☐ Fear
☐ Anxiety ☐ Strength ☐ Bravery ☐ Love ☐ Excitement ☐ Vulnerability
☐ _____   ☐ _____   ☐ _____

Sketch a scene or image from this dream:

DREAM INTERPRETATION

What does this dream make you think of from your waking life?

_____

_____

_____

When was the last time you felt the primary emotion(s) from your dream in your waking life?_____

_____

_____

Choose a few symbols to investigate in the dream dictionary or online:

SYMBOL   MEANING

_____   _____

_____   _____

_____   _____

What is your interpretation of the dream? (In words, pictures or symbols)

Have you had this dream before? ☐ Yes ☐ No ☐ Do not know
                              ☐ Recurs often ☐ Recurs occasionally

Was this dream significant in meaning to you?
☐ Very meaningful ☐ Somewhat meaningful ☐ Not at all meaningful

Are there any actions you will take based on this dream in your waking life?

1. _____

2. _____

3. _____

DREAM REMEMBRANCE

Dream Name: _____   Date: _____

First words/biggest impressions that come to mind from this dream:

_____   _____   _____

_____   _____   _____

_____   _____   _____

_____   _____   _____

Dream Summary: _____

_____

_____

_____

_____

_____

_____

_____

Primary emotion in this dream: ☐ Happiness ☐ Sadness ☐ Fear
☐ Anxiety ☐ Strength ☐ Bravery ☐ Love ☐ Excitement ☐ Vulnerability
☐ _____   ☐ _____   ☐ _____

Sketch a scene or image from this dream:

DREAM INTERPRETATION

What does this dream make you think of from your waking life?

_____
_____
_____

When was the last time you felt the primary emotion(s) from your dream in your waking life?_____

_____
_____

Choose a few symbols to investigate in the dream dictionary or online:

SYMBOL   MEANING

_____   _____
_____   _____
_____   _____

What is your interpretation of the dream? (In words, pictures or symbols)

Have you had this dream before? ☐ Yes ☐ No ☐ Do not know
                                ☐ Recurs often ☐ Recurs occasionally

Was this dream significant in meaning to you?
☐ Very meaningful ☐ Somewhat meaningful ☐ Not at all meaningful

Are there any actions you will take based on this dream in your waking life?
1. _____
2. _____
3. _____

DREAM REMEMBRANCE

Dream Name: _____   Date: _____

First words/biggest impressions that come to mind from this dream:

_____   _____   _____
_____   _____   _____
_____   _____   _____
_____   _____   _____

Dream Summary: _____

_____
_____
_____
_____
_____
_____
_____

Primary emotion in this dream: ☐ Happiness ☐ Sadness ☐ Fear
☐ Anxiety ☐ Strength ☐ Bravery ☐ Love ☐ Excitement ☐ Vulnerability
☐ _____   ☐ _____   ☐ _____

Sketch a scene or image from this dream:

DREAM INTERPRETATION

What does this dream make you think of from your waking life?

_____

_____

_____

When was the last time you felt the primary emotion(s) from your dream in your waking life?_____

_____

_____

Choose a few symbols to investigate in the dream dictionary or online:

SYMBOL   MEANING

_____   _____

_____   _____

_____   _____

What is your interpretation of the dream? (In words, pictures or symbols)

Have you had this dream before? ☐Yes ☐ No ☐ Do not know
☐ Recurs often ☐ Recurs occasionally

Was this dream significant in meaning to you?
☐Very meaningful ☐Somewhat meaningful ☐Not at all meaningful

Are there any actions you will take based on this dream in your waking life?
1. _____
2. _____
3. _____

DREAM REMEMBRANCE

Dream Name: _____   Date: _____

First words/biggest impressions that come to mind from this dream:

_____   _____   _____
_____   _____   _____
_____   _____   _____
_____   _____   _____

Dream Summary: _____
_____
_____
_____
_____
_____
_____
_____

Primary emotion in this dream: ☐ Happiness ☐ Sadness ☐ Fear
☐ Anxiety ☐ Strength ☐ Bravery ☐ Love ☐ Excitement ☐ Vulnerability
☐ _____   ☐ _____   ☐ _____

Sketch a scene or image from this dream:

DREAM INTERPRETATION

What does this dream make you think of from your waking life?

_____
_____
_____

When was the last time you felt the primary emotion(s) from your dream in your waking life?_____
_____
_____

Choose a few symbols to investigate in the dream dictionary or online:

SYMBOL   MEANING

_____   _____
_____   _____
_____   _____

What is your interpretation of the dream? (In words, pictures or symbols)

```



```

Have you had this dream before? ☐Yes ☐ No ☐ Do not know
                              ☐ Recurs often ☐ Recurs occasionally

Was this dream significant in meaning to you?
☐Very meaningful ☐Somewhat meaningful ☐Not at all meaningful

Are there any actions you will take based on this dream in your waking life?
1. _____
2. _____
3. _____

DREAM REMEMBRANCE

Dream Name: _____   Date: _____

First words/biggest impressions that come to mind from this dream:

_____   _____   _____
_____   _____   _____
_____   _____   _____
_____   _____   _____

Dream Summary: _____

_____
_____
_____
_____
_____
_____
_____

Primary emotion in this dream: ☐ Happiness ☐ Sadness ☐ Fear
☐ Anxiety ☐ Strength ☐ Bravery ☐ Love ☐ Excitement ☐ Vulnerability
☐ _____   ☐ _____   ☐ _____

Sketch a scene or image from this dream:

DREAM INTERPRETATION

What does this dream make you think of from your waking life?

_____

_____

_____

When was the last time you felt the primary emotion(s) from your dream in your waking life?_____

_____

_____

Choose a few symbols to investigate in the dream dictionary or online:

SYMBOL   MEANING

_____   _____

_____   _____

_____   _____

What is your interpretation of the dream? (In words, pictures or symbols)

Have you had this dream before? ☐Yes ☐ No ☐ Do not know
                                                    ☐ Recurs often ☐ Recurs occasionally

Was this dream significant in meaning to you?
☐Very meaningful ☐Somewhat meaningful ☐Not at all meaningful

Are there any actions you will take based on this dream in your waking life?
1. _____
2. _____
3. _____

DREAM REMEMBRANCE

Dream Name: _____   Date: _____

First words/biggest impressions that come to mind from this dream:

_____   _____   _____
_____   _____   _____
_____   _____   _____
_____   _____   _____

Dream Summary: _____

_____
_____
_____
_____
_____
_____
_____

Primary emotion in this dream: ☐ Happiness ☐ Sadness ☐ Fear
☐ Anxiety ☐ Strength ☐ Bravery ☐ Love ☐ Excitement ☐ Vulnerability
☐ _____   ☐ _____   ☐ _____

Sketch a scene or image from this dream:

DREAM INTERPRETATION

What does this dream make you think of from your waking life?

_____

_____

_____

When was the last time you felt the primary emotion(s) from your dream in your waking life?_____

_____

_____

Choose a few symbols to investigate in the dream dictionary or online:

SYMBOL   MEANING

_____   _____

_____   _____

_____   _____

What is your interpretation of the dream? (In words, pictures or symbols)

Have you had this dream before? ☐Yes ☐ No ☐ Do not know
☐ Recurs often ☐ Recurs occasionally

Was this dream significant in meaning to you?
☐Very meaningful ☐Somewhat meaningful ☐Not at all meaningful

Are there any actions you will take based on this dream in your waking life?
1. _____
2. _____
3. _____

DREAM REMEMBRANCE

Dream Name: _____   Date: _____

First words/biggest impressions that come to mind from this dream:

_____   _____   _____

_____   _____   _____

_____   _____   _____

_____   _____   _____

Dream Summary: _____

_____

_____

_____

_____

_____

_____

_____

Primary emotion in this dream: ☐ Happiness ☐ Sadness ☐ Fear
☐ Anxiety ☐ Strength ☐ Bravery ☐ Love ☐ Excitement ☐ Vulnerability
☐ _____   ☐ _____   ☐ _____

Sketch a scene or image from this dream:

DREAM INTERPRETATION

What does this dream make you think of from your waking life?

_____

_____

_____

When was the last time you felt the primary emotion(s) from your dream in your waking life?_____

_____

_____

Choose a few symbols to investigate in the dream dictionary or online:

SYMBOL   MEANING

_____   _____

_____   _____

_____   _____

What is your interpretation of the dream? (In words, pictures or symbols)

Have you had this dream before? ☐Yes ☐ No ☐ Do not know
                              ☐ Recurs often ☐ Recurs occasionally

Was this dream significant in meaning to you?
☐Very meaningful ☐Somewhat meaningful ☐Not at all meaningful

Are there any actions you will take based on this dream in your waking life?
1. _____
2. _____
3. _____

DREAM REMEMBRANCE

Dream Name: _____   Date: _____

First words/biggest impressions that come to mind from this dream:

_____   _____   _____

_____   _____   _____

_____   _____   _____

_____   _____   _____

Dream Summary: _____

_____

_____

_____

_____

_____

_____

_____

Primary emotion in this dream: ☐ Happiness ☐ Sadness ☐ Fear
☐ Anxiety ☐ Strength ☐ Bravery ☐ Love ☐ Excitement ☐ Vulnerability
☐ _____   ☐ _____   ☐ _____

Sketch a scene or image from this dream:

DREAM INTERPRETATION

What does this dream make you think of from your waking life?

_____

_____

_____

When was the last time you felt the primary emotion(s) from your dream in your waking life?_____

_____

_____

Choose a few symbols to investigate in the dream dictionary or online:

SYMBOL   MEANING

_____   _____

_____   _____

_____   _____

What is your interpretation of the dream? (In words, pictures or symbols)

Have you had this dream before? ☐Yes ☐ No ☐ Do not know

☐ Recurs often ☐ Recurs occasionally

Was this dream significant in meaning to you?
☐Very meaningful ☐Somewhat meaningful ☐Not at all meaningful

Are there any actions you will take based on this dream in your waking life?

1. _____

2. _____

3. _____

DREAM REMEMBRANCE

Dream Name: _____   Date: _____

First words/biggest impressions that come to mind from this dream:

_____   _____   _____
_____   _____   _____
_____   _____   _____
_____   _____   _____

Dream Summary: _____

_____
_____
_____
_____
_____
_____
_____

Primary emotion in this dream: ☐ Happiness ☐ Sadness ☐ Fear
☐ Anxiety ☐ Strength ☐ Bravery ☐ Love ☐ Excitement ☐ Vulnerability
☐ _____   ☐ _____   ☐ _____

Sketch a scene or image from this dream:

DREAM INTERPRETATION

What does this dream make you think of from your waking life?

_____

_____

_____

When was the last time you felt the primary emotion(s) from your dream in your waking life?_____

_____

_____

Choose a few symbols to investigate in the dream dictionary or online:

SYMBOL   MEANING

_____   _____

_____   _____

_____   _____

What is your interpretation of the dream? (In words, pictures or symbols)

Have you had this dream before? ☐ Yes ☐ No ☐ Do not know

☐ Recurs often ☐ Recurs occasionally

Was this dream significant in meaning to you?

☐ Very meaningful ☐ Somewhat meaningful ☐ Not at all meaningful

Are there any actions you will take based on this dream in your waking life?

1. _____

2. _____

3. _____

DREAM REMEMBRANCE

Dream Name: _____   Date: _____

First words/biggest impressions that come to mind from this dream:

_____   _____   _____

_____   _____   _____

_____   _____   _____

_____   _____   _____

Dream Summary: _____

_____

_____

_____

_____

_____

_____

_____

Primary emotion in this dream: ☐ Happiness ☐ Sadness ☐ Fear
☐ Anxiety ☐ Strength ☐ Bravery ☐ Love ☐ Excitement ☐ Vulnerability
☐ _____   ☐ _____   ☐ _____

Sketch a scene or image from this dream:

DREAM INTERPRETATION

What does this dream make you think of from your waking life?

_____

_____

_____

When was the last time you felt the primary emotion(s) from your dream in your waking life?_____

_____

_____

Choose a few symbols to investigate in the dream dictionary or online:

SYMBOL   MEANING

_____   _____

_____   _____

_____   _____

What is your interpretation of the dream? (In words, pictures or symbols)

Have you had this dream before? ☐ Yes ☐ No ☐ Do not know
                              ☐ Recurs often ☐ Recurs occasionally

Was this dream significant in meaning to you?
☐ Very meaningful ☐ Somewhat meaningful ☐ Not at all meaningful

Are there any actions you will take based on this dream in your waking life?
  1. _____
  2. _____
  3. _____

DREAM REMEMBRANCE

Dream Name: _____   Date: _____

First words/biggest impressions that come to mind from this dream:

_____   _____   _____

_____   _____   _____

_____   _____   _____

_____   _____   _____

Dream Summary: _____

_____

_____

_____

_____

_____

_____

_____

Primary emotion in this dream: ☐ Happiness ☐ Sadness ☐ Fear
☐ Anxiety ☐ Strength ☐ Bravery ☐ Love ☐ Excitement ☐ Vulnerability
☐ _____   ☐ _____   ☐ _____

Sketch a scene or image from this dream:

DREAM INTERPRETATION

What does this dream make you think of from your waking life?

_____

_____

_____

When was the last time you felt the primary emotion(s) from your dream in your waking life?_____

_____

_____

Choose a few symbols to investigate in the dream dictionary or online:

SYMBOL   MEANING

_____   _____

_____   _____

_____   _____

What is your interpretation of the dream? (In words, pictures or symbols)

```




```

Have you had this dream before? ☐ Yes ☐ No ☐ Do not know

☐ Recurs often ☐ Recurs occasionally

Was this dream significant in meaning to you?

☐ Very meaningful ☐ Somewhat meaningful ☐ Not at all meaningful

Are there any actions you will take based on this dream in your waking life?

1. _____

2. _____

3. _____

DREAM REMEMBRANCE

Dream Name: _____   Date: _____

First words/biggest impressions that come to mind from this dream:

_____   _____   _____
_____   _____   _____
_____   _____   _____
_____   _____   _____

Dream Summary: _____
_____
_____
_____
_____
_____
_____
_____

Primary emotion in this dream: ☐ Happiness ☐ Sadness ☐ Fear
☐ Anxiety ☐ Strength ☐ Bravery ☐ Love ☐ Excitement ☐ Vulnerability
☐ _____   ☐ _____   ☐ _____

Sketch a scene or image from this dream:

DREAM INTERPRETATION

What does this dream make you think of from your waking life?

_____
_____
_____

When was the last time you felt the primary emotion(s) from your dream in your waking life?_____

_____
_____

Choose a few symbols to investigate in the dream dictionary or online:

SYMBOL   MEANING

_____   _____
_____   _____
_____   _____

What is your interpretation of the dream? (In words, pictures or symbols)

```

```

Have you had this dream before? ☐Yes ☐ No ☐ Do not know
☐ Recurs often ☐ Recurs occasionally

Was this dream significant in meaning to you?
☐Very meaningful ☐Somewhat meaningful ☐Not at all meaningful

Are there any actions you will take based on this dream in your waking life?
1._____
2._____
3._____

DREAM REMEMBRANCE

Dream Name: _____   Date: _____

First words/biggest impressions that come to mind from this dream:

_____   _____   _____

_____   _____   _____

_____   _____   _____

_____   _____   _____

Dream Summary: _____

_____

_____

_____

_____

_____

_____

_____

Primary emotion in this dream: ☐ Happiness ☐ Sadness ☐ Fear
☐ Anxiety ☐ Strength ☐ Bravery ☐ Love ☐ Excitement ☐ Vulnerability
☐ _____   ☐ _____   ☐ _____

Sketch a scene or image from this dream:

DREAM INTERPRETATION

What does this dream make you think of from your waking life?

_____

_____

_____

When was the last time you felt the primary emotion(s) from your dream in your waking life?_____

_____

_____

Choose a few symbols to investigate in the dream dictionary or online:

SYMBOL   MEANING

_____   _____

_____   _____

_____   _____

What is your interpretation of the dream? (In words, pictures or symbols)

Have you had this dream before? ☐Yes ☐ No ☐ Do not know
☐ Recurs often ☐ Recurs occasionally

Was this dream significant in meaning to you?
☐Very meaningful ☐Somewhat meaningful ☐Not at all meaningful

Are there any actions you will take based on this dream in your waking life?
1. _____
2. _____
3. _____

9 DREAM INTERPRETATION INDEX

WELCOME THE THE DREAM INTERPRETATION index of this dream journal. In this section, we have listed 100+ common dream symbols in alphabetical order. Look up the symbols that you feel most strongly from your dreams, and see if you can connect their common interpretation to a situation from your waking life.

Dream Symbols

Age: If you dream that you are young, this dream may represent lost opportunity. Or, just dreaming of yourself being a different age may mean that is the true age that you see yourself as.

Anger: Expressing anger in a dream symbolizes frustrations and disappointments in yourself.

Animals: Generally, animals represent the animal nature within all of us. It can mean something that cannot be tamed or controlled.

Apocalypse: This may mean you are feeling especially vulnerable at the moment.

Babies: Can symbolize a desire to produce offspring, or symbolize an aspect of your own vulnerability or need to feel loved. Babies can also signify a new start or something new entering into your life.

Barefoot: Symbolizes a playful attitude and a relaxed, carefree mindset. Depending on the setting, being barefoot could also indicate poverty, lack of mobility, or misunderstanding.

Beaches: Usually symbolize the unconscious mind and our emotions. They can be a metaphor for the transition between the conscious and the unconscious.

Bears: Can mean independence, renewal and strength. Symbolize the cyclical nature of life.

Birds: Symbolizes hopes and goals. Also means joy, happiness, sunshine and a positive outlook on life.

Bisexual: Even if you do not identify as bisexual in your waking life, this dream may tell you that there is some aspect of your sexuality that you are questioning.

Blood: Symbolizes life, fluidity, passion and that which nourishes us. Blood dreams deal with the essentials of emotional issues.

Body: Represents our dreaming mind in terms of stability, action, knowledge, and structure. These dreams may also be indicative of health and health-related issues.

Bouncing: In some dreams this is a lead-up to a lucid dreaming experience (When you are conscious you are dreaming within a dream). It can also symbolize exhilaration or sexual excitement.

Buildings: Buildings are symbolic of our bodies and the condition of the building signifies our current status, whether emotional, mental, spiritual or physical. Alternatively, buildings may also point to social status.

Butterflies: Signify longevity, creativity, romance and spirituality. You may be experiencing a new way of thinking, or you are undergoing some sort of transformation.

Cat: Cats often represent femininity and softness in a dream. They can also point to deceit or creativity.

Celebrity: Meeting a celebrity in a dream can point to what talents you believe are important, and can show a desire for recognition.

Chased: Can symbolize a problem that might be hanging over your head and now's the time to finally face it.

Cheating: This can mean that there are trust issues you are experiencing in your waking life.

Choking: Often indicates a fearful experience. Choking on an object suggests that you may find some advice or situation difficult to accept. Alternatively, you may feel that you are unable to completely express yourself.

Dark figure: Symbolizes a fear of the future and your anxiety in facing this fear.

Death of a Loved One: Symbolizes a missing aspect or quality of your life that goes unrecognized and can lead you to changes in your life.

Death, General: Symbolizes a wish to end something in the dreamer's life such as a relationship of some sort.

Death, Near-Death Experience: A near-death experience implies that you are experiencing a kind of relapse. You are reverting back to old habits and ways. It also may indicate that you are being given a second chance.

Dog: Dogs in dreams point to loyalty, friends, and the idea of the protector. In some cases, the dog means to represent you, but in other cases, someone close to you (past or present) may be symbolized by the dog.

Dreaming Within a Dream: Excessively worried and fearful about a situation or circumstance that you are going through. Serves as a layer of protection.

Driving Recklessly: Warning from your subconscious about your habits. Watch bad habits as they may become long-term problems.

Driving: Can represent the control you have over where you are going in your waking life.

Drowning: Symbolizes that your emotions are overwhelming you; you are being helplessly submerged in them.

Eagle: An eagle points to nobility and bravery. It also has a spiritual side, and may show you your deepest desires of what you want to achieve.

Elevator: Going down symbolizes something negative. Going up may represent a promotion at work or good fortune. And if the elevator is stuck it can mean stagnation and being confined and oppressed.

Falling: Can mean a loss of control, insecurity, or reckless behaviour.

Fish (Rotting or Smelly): Denotes distress that will come in the disguise of happiness.

Fish: To see fish swimming signifies intuitions from your subconscious mind that you can't quite grasp. Thus to catch a fish represents insights which have been brought to the surface.

Floating: Can mean independence or success. Often related to feelings of positive emotions.

Flying: Signifies a sense of freedom where you had initially felt restricted or incomplete.

Friendship, Old Friend: This symbol depends on the relationship you had with this person, but it usually represents longing for a peaceful time with less stress in your life.

Gate: A barrier or an entrance. Signifying either new beginnings or the end to something significant. Whether the gate is locked or unlocked determines your emotional state.

Giant: Signifies insurmountable struggles in your waking hours. If you can defeat the giant, it means that success is coming to you.

Gun: Represents the need for protection or anxiety about something. The gun's symbolism is masculine-dominant and tends towards aggression.

Hair: A full head of healthy, lustrous hair is typically a sign of virility, while balding is a sign of insecurity or possible low libido or anger.

Hands: The left hand denotes the feminine; the right symbolizes the masculine. In other terms, the left hand can be a symbol for something you receive, and the right hand a symbol of something you are giving away or projecting. Injuring your hand can mean a blow to your ego.

Hang Gliding: Symbolizes freedom in your personal life. It also represents trust. You believe in destiny.

Hat: A hat means that something is being hidden. Often, it is a part of yourself that you are keeping out of view of others.

Hermaphrodite: Represents the union of opposites, balance, and ambiguity. Alternatively, the dreams suggest that you may be trying to conceal your sexuality.

Horseback Riding: Indicates that you are in a position of power. You have confidence in your ability. Alternatively, the dream represents your lack of integrity.

Illness: Signifies some aspect of your conviction that you might not be aware of; it may also mean you are without clarity in your spiritual life. It may also point to feelings of abandonment.

Insects: Generally symbolize a disagreeable feeling, emotion or some sort of overwhelming struggle.

Juggling: This symbol, whether you are juggling or watching someone else juggle in your dream, means that you have too much going on at once, and you worry you cannot manage it all. If the juggler drops something, it was warning that bad things could happen if you do not get all these different things under control.

Jumping: Indicates that you need to take a risk and go for it. You will overcome your obstacles and find progress toward your goals.

Killing: You may be releasing repressed rage towards someone or something, possibly even yourself. You may want to end to your relationship with the object being murdered.

Ladder: Ladders represent a desire to reach higher levels in any given area of your life.

Lateness: Symbolizes that you are overwhelmed and could be dealing with too much stress in your personal life.

Laughing: Whether you are laughing yourself or just hearing the laughter of someone else, this can indicate that you are taking an aspect of your life too seriously, and would benefit from lightening up a bit.

Lottery: Winning the lottery represents a strong desire to be free from financial concerns.

Lover: Represents the relationship with your own nature and symbolizes how you see yourself.

Magic: Symbolizes creativity and scope of vision, unexpected changes, and power; seeing a magic event alludes to good fortune will come your way.

Mirror: A mirror may indicate that you are too focused on how others perceive you, if you can see your reflection. If there is a mirror, but you cannot see your reflection, it can mean that you are not being true to yourself, and do not understand your own identity.

Money (General): Can symbolize an exchange of value, or how much you think something in your life is worth, whether spiritual, emotional or actual currency.

Money (Winning Great Fortune): Indicates that success and prosperity within your reach.

Mugged or Robbed: Being mugged suggests that you are suffering from an identity crisis. Perhaps you have done something or are being asked to do something that is out of character.

Neighbor: If you see one of your neighbors in your dream, or dream about being neighbors with someone, it can symbolize your home life. A friendly neighbor points to peace and tranquility, while an upset neighbor means an unhappy home in some way.

Nudity: Represents vulnerability an anxiety if you are naked. If you see another person naked that can mean an openly expressed aspect of that person.

Owl: An owl is a common dream symbol that points to wisdom and new knowledge.

Pain: If you dream of pain, it can mean you are too hard on yourself in some aspect of your life.

Paralysis: This typically epitomizes feeling trapped. It could also represent an inability to express your feeling to others in ways they'll understand.

Phone (Ringing): Your subconscious is trying to reach out to you, and it is imperative that you listen to your underlying feelings.

Pregnancy: Represents a need to start a creative project or the need to generate new ideas.

Pregnancy: The birth of a new stage in your life, new ideas, fresh starts, new goals, or new beginnings. Maybe something in your life is growing or being nurtured.

Radio: Symbolizes of connection and communication. You might want to get in contact with a long-lost friend.

Rain: Rain may mean tears, but those tears may also be leading to a renewal and a fresh start. It is almost like becoming clean with the water.

Roads: Show the direction you are headed generally in life. You may be heading toward another dream symbol, or perhaps trying to escape one in your past. These dreams can give you clues as to what to focus on in your waking life.

Running: When dreaming of running away from someone this might indicate avoidance of an issue.

Scale: A scale points to an upcoming difficult decision in your life. You should "weigh" your options from new perspectives.

School: Often times represents your work environment

Screaming , Trying but Unable to: Indicates your sense of helplessness and frustration in some situation.

Screaming: Symbolizes deep set anger, fear, and/or frustration at someone or towards yourself; the expression of a powerful emotion which you have kept pent up inside.

Sex: Refers to the integration of different qualities in yourself that can feel conflicting or opposites. It represents psychological merging.

Speaking, Cannot: The inability to speak or call out in a dream can represent being afraid that your opinions or voice isn't being heard in some particular area of your life.

Steps: Whether you are going up or down is important, as it could mean loss or gain. Steps usually represent your financial position or social status in life, so it may mean gains in these areas or losses.

Swimming: Suggests that you are exploring aspects of your subconscious mind and emotions

Teeth Falling Out: this meaning can vary greatly but can symbolize losing confidence. In general terms it's a strong indication or representation of problems in your life.

Test-Taking: Failing to prepare for a school exam is an extremely common dream that follow people their whole life. It often signifies anxiety about an upcoming event or aspect of your life.

Underwater: Represents a need for greater control of your life. Being underwater suggests that you are overwhelmed and under a lot of pressure.

Vampire: A vampire can point to sensuality on one hand, but death on the other. Often, it means someone we are drawn to, even if we know that person is not good for us.

War: This shows that your life is feeling chaotic at the moment. You may be experiencing conflicts within yourself, that are causing you harm.

Water, Large Body of Open Water: Represents the unknown. It suggests that you can't see the future clearly; the weather conditions symbolize other feelings towards the situation.

Whirlwind: Wind, tornados or hurricanes can mean chaos, confusion and perhaps even scandal. The dream can also mean that you are being pulled in a certain direction against your will.

Wind Chimes: Symbolize harmony and tranquility. Alternatively, wind chimes represent past memories.

Windows: Signify hopes, vast possibilities and insight; the size of the window is reflective of your outlook. A small window suggests that you tend to be pessimistic, and a large window symbolizes optimism.

"X" (Letter): Seeing the letter "x" or an "x" drawn across something means something that is forbidden. Maybe it is something you are trying to forbid yourself from, or someone else is trying to stop you from being involved in.

Yelling: Represents repressed anger that needs to be expressed in your waking life.

Dream Colors

Black: Black can represent a person's unconscious, or it can mean looking inside yourself to transform, to be born anew. In some cases, moving into blackness or darkness means that you are going through a period of change, or you feel threatened.

Blue: Blue points to peace and tranquility. It can also mean a need for rest, or to feel secure in a trusting relationship.

Purple: Purple in dreams usually points to something mystical or magical. It can be a blissful state, an intuition, or union with another person.

Gray: Gray means neutrality. It means you are staying out of it — whatever "it" may be. You are not taking sides, and you re trying to protect your emotions.

Green: The color green is all about control. Green shows a desire to control events, the future, and having a desire for security, certainty, and recognition.

White: White in dreams means newness. This may be a new beginning, a new perspective, or even new feelings.

Orange: Orange shows new-found freedom, or a desire to connect more closely with other people. It can also mean a general feeling of restlessness.

Red: Red shows intensity, and a desire to feel assertive. It can also point to injury or sexual desire.

Yellow: Yellow in dreams shows a desire for resolution. You are seeking closure in something, want to tie up loose ends, or are feeling uncertain about the future.

10 CONCLUSION

THANK YOU FOR READING THIS book about dream interpretation and analysis, and I hope that it has revealed some interesting insights to you about your subconscious and your true feelings. By now, you should have a good understanding of how to better remember your dreams and interpret them, as well as access to a 100+ list of dream symbols and their corresponding meanings.

I hope that you have many dream-filled nights ahead of you, ready to interpret and learn about it in the morning, and I hope this dream journal has helped you in that quest.

Thanks for reading!

Your Feedback is Important to Me

Dear Reader,

Thank you for taking the time to read this book. I hope you got a lot out of it and learned something you can apply to your own life.

If you have any feedback, positive or negative, I'd love to hear from you. I personally read all the reviews on my Amazon page, and hope you'll take a minute to tell me (and other readers) what you think.

Type this URL into your browser to go straight to the review page for this book: bitly.com/dreamjournalreview

Thank you!

—Rozella Hart

Printed in Great Britain
by Amazon

32920546R00070